P9-DMV-171

BLAZERS

U.S. MILITARY
SUBMARINES

by Barbara Alpert

CONTENT CONSULTANT:
RAYMOND L. PUFFER, PHD
HISTORIAN, RET.
EDWARDS AIR FORCE BASE HISTORY OFFICE

READING CONSULTANT:
BARBARA J. FOX
READING SPECIALIST
PROFESSOR EMERITA
NORTH CAROLINA STATE UNIVERSITY

CAPSTONE PRESS
a capstone imprint

Blazers is published by Capstone Press,
1710 Roe Crest Drive, North Mankato, Minnesota 56003.
www.capstonepub.com

Library of Congress Cataloging-in-Publication Data
Alpert, Barbara.
　　U.S. military submarines / by Barbara Alpert.
　　p. cm. — (Capstone blazers: U.S. military technology)
　　Includes bibliographical references and index.
　　ISBN 978-1-4296-8440-8 (library binding)
　　　ISBN 978-1-62065-212-1 (ebook PDF)
1. Submarines (Ships)—United States—Juvenile literature. I. Title.
V858.A742 2013
3559.9'3830973—dc23   2012001000

Summary: Describes the submarines used by the U.S. military.

Editorial Credits

Brenda Haugen, editor; Kyle Grenz, designer; Laura Manthe, production specialist

Photo Credits

Photo courtesy of General Dynamics Electric Boat, 14-15, 17 (top); U.S. Navy photo, cover
(bottom), 5, 10-11, 28, by Jeremy Lambert, 17 (bottom), JO1 Jason E. Miller, 26-27, JO3 Wes
Eplen, cover (top), JOSN Brandon Shelander, 9, Lt. Rebecca Rebarich, 21, MC2 Gretchen M.
Albrecht, 22-23, MC2 Kimberly Clifford, 18, MCSA Cameron Bramham, 12-13, PH2 Eric S.
Logsdon, 29, PH2 Todd Cichonowicz, 25, SKC Michael Murphy, 6-7

Artistic Effects

deviantart.com/Salwiak, backgrounds

Printed in the United States of America in
Stevens Point, Wisconsin.
032012   006678WZF12

TABLE OF CONTENTS

BATTLE READY

For years battles were fought on the ocean's surface. But what if sailors could surprise an enemy by sailing underwater? Submarines answered this question.

To dive under the surface, submarines (subs) fill tanks with water. To make subs rise, air pushes water out of the tanks.

SUBMARINE CROSS SECTION

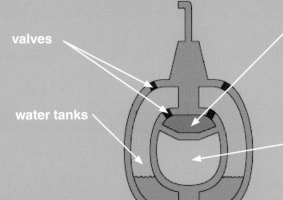

valves

compressed
air tanks

water tanks

interior
(the inside of
a submarine
where the crew
lives and works)

CHAPTER 1

UNDERWATER WARFARE

Most subs are powered by steam. This steam spins the sub's **propellers**. Subs use **sonar** to find their way in dark water and locate enemy ships.

sonar screen

propeller—a rotating blade that moves a vehicle through water

sonar—a device that uses sound waves to find underwater objects

 Sonar sends out sound waves. The sound waves bounce off objects and show where the targets are located.

When a sub is under water, sailors use a periscope to see above the water.

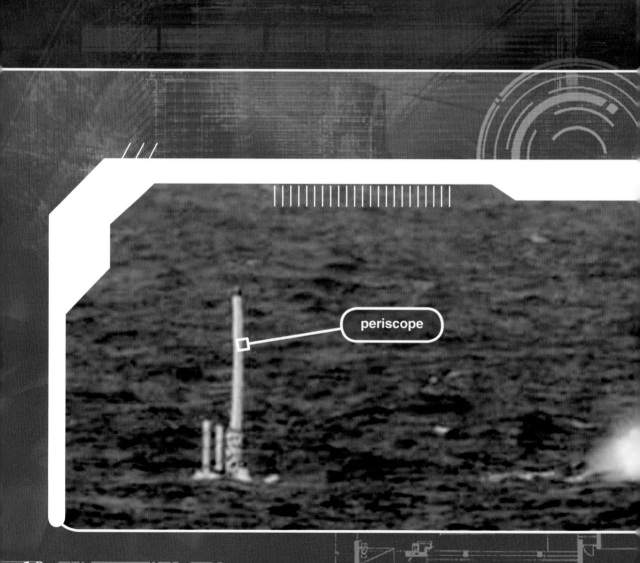

periscope

Subs are nearly invisible as they move beneath the ocean. They sneak up on the enemy and fire weapons.

CHAPTER 2

SURPRISE ATTACK!

Fast attack subs chase and destroy enemy submarines. A Los Angeles-**class** sub is longer than a football field. It can carry nearly 150 sailors.

WARNING₂₀₀

class—a group of submarines that have the same design

**FACT**

In a sub's control room, officers map the sub's course. They also direct the sub to dive or rise.

Seawolf-class fast attack subs are quicker and quieter than Los Angeles subs. The USS *Jimmy Carter* is 453 feet (138 meters) long. This is 100 feet (30 m) longer than other fast attack subs.

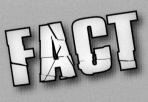

The USS *Jimmy Carter* is named for President Jimmy Carter. He was the only president to graduate from the Naval Academy.

CHAPTER 3

MISSION: SPECIAL OPS

The newest subs are called Virginia-class. These subs are 377 feet (115 m) long and carry a crew of nearly 135 sailors. The subs' **masts** use cameras to spy on ships.

mast—a tall pole on a submarine or ship

masts

Guided missile subs carry up to 150 **missiles**. These subs also bring Navy SEALs to battle zones.

Navy SEALs are some of the best fighters. Sailors must pass many mental and physical tests to become SEALs.

missile—an explosive weapon that can travel long distances

CHAPTER 4

THE BOOMERS

Ballistic missile subs are nearly 560 feet (171 m) long. This is longer than other classes of subs. They have **launch** platforms for long-range missiles. These subs are nicknamed boomers.

launch—to send off or throw

launch
platforms

Each boomer is named for a U.S. state except for one. The USS *Henry M. Jackson* is named for a U.S. senator. He believed using subs was one of the best ways to defend the country.

Boomers stay at sea up to 77 days. Each boomer has two crews. When one crew runs the boomer at sea, the other crew stays on shore.

CHAPTER 5

EMERGENCY RESCUE

If a sub crashes or suffers an explosion, its crew radios for help. The sub may lose power, flood with water, or stop making fresh air for the crew.

DSRV

A deep submergence rescue vehicle (DSRV) hurries to a damaged sub. The DSRV latches onto the sub's exit **hatch**. It can rescue up to 24 sailors at a time.

hatch—a doorway of a submarine

Special escape suits help crews survive disasters. The suits work up to 600 feet (183 m) underwater.

CHAPTER 6

SUBS OF THE FUTURE

A new shallow water combat submersible (SWCS) is being tested. This mini-sub will deliver Navy SEALs to their missions.

SWCS

GLOSSARY

WARNING 200

class (KLAS)—a group of submarines that have the same design

compressed air tank (kuhm-PREST AYR TANGK)—a container that holds air that is under pressure greater than that of the atmosphere

hatch (HACH)—a doorway of a submarine

interior (in-TIHR-ee-ur)—the inside of something

launch (LAWNCH)—to send off or throw

mast (MAST)—a tall pole on a submarine or ship

missile (MISS-uhl)—an explosive weapon that can travel long distances

Naval Academy (NAY-vuhl uh-KAD-uh-mee)—a school for training people to become officers in the U.S. Navy

propeller (pruh-PEL-ur)—a rotating blade that moves a vehicle through water

sonar (SOH-nar)—a device that uses sound waves to find underwater objects

valve (VALV)—a movable part that controls the flow of liquid or gas through a pipe

READ MORE

Jackson, Kay. *Navy Submarines in Action.* Amazing Military Vehicles. New York: PowerKids Press, 2009.

Loveless, Antony. *Nuclear Submariners.* World's Most Dangerous Jobs. New York: Crabtree Pub. Co., 2010.

Swanson, Jennifer. *How Submarines Work.* Mankato, Minn.: Child's World, 2012.

INTERNET SITES

FactHound offers a safe, fun way to find Internet sites related to this book. All of the sites on FactHound have been researched by our staff.

Here's all you do:

Visit *www.facthound.com*

Type in this code: 9781429684408

Super-cool stuff!

Check out projects, games and lots more at
www.capstonekids.com

INDEX